10th ANNIVERSARY EDITION

ADAM HAMILTON

THE JOURNEY

Walking the Road to Bethlehem

LEADER GUIDE

Abingdon Press | Nashville

The Journey:
Walking the Road to Bethlehem
Leader Guide

Copyright © 2011 by Abingdon Press.
All rights reserved.

ISBN: 978-1-7910-1821-4

Scripture quotations, unless otherwise indicated, are from the New Revised Standard Version of the Bible, copyrighted © 1989 by the Division of Christian Education of the National Council of the Churches of Christ in the United States of America, and are used by permission.

21 22 23 24 25 26 27 28 29 30 — 10 9 8 7 6 5 4 3 2 1
MANUFACTURED IN THE UNITED STATES OF AMERICA

Contents

How to Use
This Leader Guide

The aim of this study, like the aim of the book upon which it is based, is to help you better understand the events that led up to the birth of Jesus in a stable in Bethlehem; to see more clearly the theological significance of the Nativity; and to reflect upon the meaning of these events for your life.

This five-session study is made up of several components:

- the book, *The Journey: Walking the Road to Bethlehem*
- a devotional book, *The Journey: A Season of Reflections*, which provides daily devotions to accompany the book
- videos in which Adam Hamilton visits the Holy Land to retrace the steps of Mary, Joseph, and others culminating in the events around Jesus' birth
- this leader guide

Participants may choose to read the book and devotional book before or after the group session. Ideally, participants should have the opportunity to receive copies of the books prior to your first group session. If this is not possible, introduce them to the books during your first group session and try to obtain copies before your second session.

A video will be shown during each group session. You'll find more information below about use of the videos.

Using these program components, you will lead the members of your group over the course of five sessions to examine the geographical, cultural, and historical setting of the events that resulted in the birth of the Christ Child and, ultimately, to help participants see themselves in the story.

The focal Scripture texts will be Luke and Matthew's accounts of the Annunciation, Mary's visit with Elizabeth, Joseph's dream of an angel, the walk to Bethlehem, and the visits of the shepherds and, later, the magi.

Session 1 focuses on Mary and the Annunciation. Session 2 on Joseph. Session 3 considers Mary's visit with Elizabeth. Session 4 looks at the actual journey to Bethlehem. Session 5 takes us to the manger and to the shepherds' fields.

Encourage everyone in your group to keep a Bible close by during the study and to bring it to each session. Matthew, Chapters 1 and 2, and Luke, Chapters 1 and 2, provide the core of the Scripture to be considered.

The Journey: Walking the Road to Bethlehem is ideal for, but not limited to, the Advent and Christmas season. It may be used as a stand-alone study for adults by Sunday school classes and other small groups, or as part of a congregational emphasis that includes studies for youth and for children, all based on Adam Hamilton's book. However you use the program, you will find some useful tools and helps online, at www.AdamHamilton.com/TheJourney.

An Overview

As group leader, your role will be to facilitate the group sessions using the books, the videos, and this leader guide. Because no two groups are alike, this guide has been designed to give you flexibility and choice in tailoring the sessions for your group. You may choose one of the following format options, or adapt these as you wish to meet the schedule and needs of your particular group. (Note: The times indicated within parentheses are merely estimates. You may move at a faster or slower pace, making adjustments as necessary to fit your schedule.)

Basic Option: 60 minutes
Opening Prayer . . . .(2 minutes)
Biblical Foundation . . . .(3 minutes)
Video Presentation . . . .(10-12 minutes)
Group Discussion . . . .(25 minutes)
Wrapping Up . . . .(10 minutes)
Closing Prayer . . . .(5 minutes)

Extended Option: 90 minutes
Opening Prayer . . . .(2 minutes)
Biblical Foundation . . . .(3 minutes)
Opening Activity . . . .(10 minutes)
Video Presentation . . . .(10-12 minutes)
Group Discussion . . . .(20 minutes)
Book Study and Discussion . . . .(15 minutes)
Bible Study and Discussion . . . .(15 minutes)
Wrapping Up . . . .(10 minutes)
Closing Prayer . . . .(5 minutes)

While you should feel free to adapt any element in this leader guide to suit the needs and schedule of your group, take time to become familiar with the session elements below. Knowing the intended purpose and description of each element will help you decide which ones and what arrangement will work best in your situation.

Opening Prayer

The prayer will usually come from the Book of Psalms and should be read aloud at the start of the group meeting. Often the psalm will be one suggested by a particular event described in the Gospel text.

Biblical Foundation

This passage is the same one that appears at the head of each chapter in the book *The Journey: Walking the Road to Bethlehem.* Invite one of your group members to read it aloud.

Opening Activity (90-minute option)

If you follow the 90-minute schedule, each lesson plan includes an activity designed to help participants reflect on the subject (event) highlighted in the session or make a connection between it and something in their own experience.

Video Presentation

Each session's video segment features Adam Hamilton speaking from one of the sites in Jerusalem traditionally associated with the events the Gospel record. Each segment runs 10 to 12 minutes and will serve as the basis of your group's discussion in a 60-minute schedule. In the 90-minute schedule, the video discussion includes additional content from the book *The Journey: Walking the Road to Bethlehem* and related Bible passages, from both the Old and New Testaments.

Each video segment features some combination of these elements: a spoken introduction and commentary by Adam Hamilton, the author and video host; one or more scenes showing Hamilton on location in Nazareth, on the road, or in Bethlehem.

Plan to preview the video segment for each session prior to your group's meeting. Make note of images, insights, or questions that occur to you and that you think may be helpful in leading discussion. In addition, you will want to become familiar with some helps in this guide for each of the videos:

- Sights: A general summary of what viewers will see in the Holy Land portions of the videos
- Insights: A selective listing of key insights excerpted from Hamilton's commentaries and on-site narrations
- Group Discussion: A set of questions for guiding group discussion after viewing the video

Note that the DVD includes a bonus feature in which Adam Hamilton discusses the Holy Land today.

Book Study and Discussion (90-minute option)

If you follow the 90-minute schedule, this section highlights key excerpts from one of the book chapters and suggests discussion questions for use with the group in response to those excerpts. The questions provided in this section are suggestions. Keep in mind that you do not have to use all the questions provided, and you can always make up your own. Discussion questions are also provided for the reflection at the end of each chapter.

Bible Study and Discussion (90-minute option)

If you follow the 90-minute schedule, this section highlights key passages of Scripture related to the book chapter and suggests discussion questions for use with the group in response to those texts.

Wrapping Up

Each session concludes with your group reflecting imaginatively on one of the events surrounding the birth of Jesus in terms of either a place or a character. For instance, imagine yourself in the humble cave that was home to Mary and her family in Nazareth or climbing the hills of Judea and seeing the Judean wilderness in the distance. Or put yourself in the sandals of Joseph as he ponders what to do when he learns of Mary's pregnancy. This section will include discussion prompts for entering into the subject or event highlighted in the session from each of these perspectives. Depending on the time you have available or the preferences of your group, you may choose to use them all or only one.

Closing Prayer

This prayer, like the opening prayer, usually comes from one of the psalms. An individual can read it, or the whole group can offer this prayer in unison.

Helpful Hints

Here are a few helpful hints for preparing and leading the group sessions:

- Become familiar with the material before the group session. If possible, watch the video segment in advance.
- Choose the various elements you will use during the group session, including the specific discussion questions you plan to cover.
- Secure a TV and DVD player in advance; oversee room setup.
- Begin and end on time.
- Be enthusiastic! Remember, you set the tone for the class.
- Create a climate of participation, encouraging individuals to participate as they feel comfortable.
- Communicate the importance of group discussions and group exercises.
- To stimulate group discussion, consider reviewing the key insights first and then asking participants to tell what they saw as the highlights of the video.
- If no one answers right away, do not be afraid of a little silence. Count to ten silently; then say something like, "Would anyone like to go first?" If no one responds, venture an answer yourself. Then ask for comments and other responses.
- Model openness as you share with the group. Group mem-

bers will follow your example. If you limit your sharing to a surface level, others will follow suit.

- Draw out participants without asking them to share what they are unwilling to share. Make eye contact with someone and say something such as, "How about someone else?"
- Encourage multiple answers or responses before moving on.
- Ask, "Why?" or "Why do you believe that?" to help continue a discussion and give it greater depth.
- Affirm others' responses with comments such as, "Great" or "Thanks" or "Good insight"—especially if this is the first time someone has spoken during the group session.
- Give everyone a chance to talk, but keep the conversation moving. Moderate to prevent a few individuals from doing all the talking.
- Monitor your own contributions. If you are doing most of the talking, back off so that you do not train the group to listen rather than speak up.
- Remember that you do not have all the answers. Your job is to keep the discussion going and encourage participation.
- Honor the time schedule. If a session is running longer than expected, get consensus from the group before continuing beyond the agreed-upon ending time.
- Consider involving group members in various aspects of the group session, such as asking for volunteers to play the video, read the prayers, say their own prayers, or read the Scripture.

1.

Mary of Nazareth

Getting Started

Session Goals

This session is intended to help participants

- Reflect on ways in which Mary was influenced by the location where she grew to adulthood
- Reflect on ways in which group members have been shaped by the locations where they grew to adulthood
- Ponder the angel's message to Mary and Mary's response to it
- Reflect on group members' willingness to submit to the will of God for their lives as they understand it

Opening Prayer

Invite group members to join with you in the following prayer for Advent. You may copy this prayer on the board or make copes for distribution in your study group. If you make copies of this prayer, encourage group members to offer the prayer each day during the season of Advent.

> *Merciful God,*
> *you sent your messengers the prophets*
> *to preach repentance and prepare the way*
> *for our salvation.*

Give us grace to heed their warnings and forsake
our sins, that we may celebrate aright the
commemoration of the Nativity,
and may await with joy the coming in
glory of Jesus Christ our Redeemer;
who lives and reigns with you and the Holy Spirit,
One God, for ever and ever.
Amen.

Biblical Foundation

In the sixth month the angel Gabriel was sent by God to a town in Galilee called Nazareth, to a virgin engaged to a man whose name was Joseph, of the house of David. The virgin's name was Mary. And he came to her and said, "Greetings, favored one! The Lord is with you." But she was much perplexed by his words and pondered what sort of greeting this might be. The angel said to her, "Do not be afraid, Mary, for you have found favor with God. And now, you will conceive in your womb and bear a son, and you will name him Jesus. He will be great, and will be called the Son of the Most High, and the Lord God will give to him the throne of his ancestor David. He will reign over the house of Jacob forever, and of his kingdom there will be no end." Mary said to the angel, "How can this be, since I am a virgin?" The angel said to her, "The Holy Spirit will come upon you, and the power of the Most High will overshadow you; therefore the child to be born will be holy; he will be called Son of God. And now, your relative Elizabeth in her old age has also conceived a son; and this is the sixth month for her who was said to be barren. For nothing will be impossible with God." Then Mary said, "Here am I, the servant of the Lord; let it be with me according to your word." Then the angel departed from her. (Luke 1:26-38)

Opening Activity

Following the opening prayer, ask group members to form teams of three and in those teams to describe briefly their hometowns or cities. Did most of the group members grow up in the city where they now live? Or is your community one where many new people have moved in recent years?

Ask team members to describe how they feel that growing up in their hometowns has affected them as adults. Do some team members still carry regional accents? regional colloquialisms? regional opinions about politics, culture, and so on? Do some team members strive to overcome their hometowns? Do others cling tenaciously to their hometowns? Some, such as persons who grew up in military families, may have no hometowns. Where and how do such persons derive an identity? What have such persons missed—or gained—by having no hometowns?

Learning Together

Video Presentation

Introduce the video for this session in these ways:

- Introduce the video presenter, Adam Hamilton, and provide some biographical information about him.
- Explain that this video was filmed at biblically and archaeologically important sites in Israel.
- If possible, post a large map of the Holy Land and point out the locations of Nazareth, Sepphoris, Jerusalem, the Sea of Galilee, and the Dead Sea. Figure the rough distances between Nazareth, Jerusalem, Bethlehem, Jericho, and other major sites. Remind group members that almost all travel was by foot over very rugged terrain.
- Invite group members to take notes as they watch the video. Listen especially for the description of Nazareth during the time of Mary and Joseph, the importance of a source of fresh water for town sites, the meaning of the name *Nazareth,* and the likely space in which Mary lived while in Nazareth.

- Invite group members to request that the video be stopped and replayed as necessary.

Play the video. Be sure that all can see and hear clearly.

Sights
- The Roman city of Sepphoris, with its cobbled streets and elaborate mosaics
- The humble village of Nazareth
- The ancient spring, still running, that provided water for the village of Nazareth
- The modern city of Nazareth, now much larger and more cosmopolitan than at the time of Mary and Joseph
- The elaborate churches and shrines built over sites believed to be the home of Mary
- The caves in which many persons in ancient Nazareth lived

Insights
- The very strong Roman influence in Sepphoris, and, to a lesser degree, in ancient Nazareth
- The absolute dependence on a source of fresh water for a town site
- The use of caves, both natural and hand-hewn, as living quarters that provided protection from the elements as well as natural cooling during the hot, dry Palestinian summers
- The simplicity of Mary's life in Nazareth
- The reality of God's plan in choosing a humble young woman in a humble community to bear the Christ Child
- The importance of the names of places and people at the time of Mary

Group Discussion
Raise these questions for discussion by the group. Do not spend too much time on any one question, and try to encourage everyone to take part in the discussion.
- What did you see in the video that surprised you or was new

to you? In what ways did these new or surprising elements help you understand God's choice of Mary in Nazareth as the mother of Jesus? What new dimensions of Mary emerge for you as a result of seeing and learning about her hometown and the way she lived?

- How do you think Mary and the other residents of Nazareth might have been affected by living so close to a wealthy Roman city—and so far from the center of her own culture, namely Jerusalem?
- What was—and continues to be—the significance of the name *Nazareth*? If the town name means branch or shoot, how does this illuminate God's choice of Nazareth as the home of the one who was to bear the Prince of Peace?

Book Study and Discussion

In Chapter 1 of *The Journey,* Adam Hamilton gives some attention to the location of Nazareth and to the meaning of the town's name. He also gives considerable attention to the angel's message to Mary (the Annunciation) and to the concept of the virgin birth, which, as Hamilton points out, might more accurately be called the virginal conception.

Divide the group into teams of four and ask each team to quickly review the chapter sections titled Mary and The Virgin Birth. Then invite the teams to consider some of these statements and questions:

- What did God demonstrate in the choice of Mary to give birth to the Messiah? Recall that Mary was what we might call a "nobody from nowhere"—that is, she was a seemingly unremarkable person from a nondescript town.
- Why didn't God choose a person of high rank from, say, Jerusalem? Recall other biblical examples of people chosen to do God's will. Which of these people were of high and noble rank, and which were ordinary and lowly?
- What does the choice of people to do God's will in biblical times suggest about who is chosen in our day?

The author points out that the angel declared Mary to be "full of grace," then goes on to say that this phrase may have given rise to the doctrine of the Immaculate Conception—the belief that Mary was conceived without the taint of original sin.

- What else might be meant by the phrase "full of grace"?
- In this passage, who or what do you think is the source of grace?
- Who is the recipient of grace?
- Could the angel have declared any others to be "full of grace?" Explain your answers.

Put yourself in Mary's shoes. Then consider one or more of these questions:

- What questions would you ask if an angel appeared to you with a word from God? (Hint: Start with "How would you know that the person was an angel from God?")
- In what ways did Mary's background prepare her for sensing an angel and listening to an angel—outlandish as the message must have seemed to her? Recall, as the author points out, that Mary was young, perhaps thirteen, and without formal education.
- Now ponder Mary's response to the angel. Was her statement an indication of resignation? enthusiastic acceptance? eagerness to obey? begrudging willingness to go along with it? something else? Give reasons for your answers.

(Don't we wish the Gospel writers had indicated inflection, expression, and emotion in their narratives!)

Ask for brief reports from the teams; focus especially on questions and concerns.

Now, in the same teams of four, move to consideration of the virgin birth.

At the outset, recognize that many Protestants confess belief in the virgin birth in the creeds or affirmations of faith used in services of worship. Both the traditional Nicene Creed and the very popular Apostles' Creed affirm the virgin birth. And yet the virgin birth has been a sticking point for many believers. To help team members consider the issue and clarify their own understandings, pose these discussion questions:

- Why do you think the virgin birth isn't mentioned in the Gospels of Mark and John? Are these Gospels less important or less reliable because they do not refer to the virgin birth? Explain your answer.
- Would Jesus still have been the Christ if he were not born of a virgin? Explain your answer.
- Should belief in and acceptance of the virgin birth be the "litmus test" of one's faith in Christ? Must all who are Christians confess the virgin birth? Why or why not?

Reassemble as a larger group and listen to brief reports from each of the teams, focusing again on questions and concerns. Do all members of all the teams hold to the same beliefs? If so, what are those beliefs? If not, is the grace of the community broad enough to accept those with doubts or with opinions contrary to the rest of the group?

Reflection

- How would you define *angel*? Do you believe in angels? Why or why not?
- Using Adam Hamilton's definition of angels as "messengers," name and describe some of the angels in your life.
- Do you think there have been times when you have failed to recognize angels who have appeared in your life? If so, describe some of those times. How might things have turned out differently if you had recognized them?
- Have there been times when you felt that, intentionally or unintentionally, you were an angel in someone's life? How do you feel about this possibility? How did the person respond?

Bible Study and Discussion

Your group members have already struggled with the meanings in the biblical passage covered in this session. Now, live that lesson vividly.

Select three strong readers—one to read the part of the angel Gabriel, one to read the part of Mary, and one to serve as narrator. These three will read Luke 1:26-38 aloud for the whole group. Encourage the readers of Mary's part and the angel Gabriel's part to read with as much expression and feeling as they can. Surely, neither Mary nor the angel spoke calmly, quietly, and without emotion; make this reading come alive!

What kind of expression should the readers use? That's up to them. Note that the narrator reads only verses 26 and 27 to set the stage; the rest is a dialogue between the angel Gabriel and Mary. Omit "The angel said to her" and "Then Mary said." The reader of Mary's part must sound perplexed and pondering, as verse 29 suggests.

Following the reading, ask group members for new insights or understandings of the angel's message (the Annunciation) that they received from hearing these words read aloud with feeling and expression.

Wrapping Up

Begin to close the session by discussing ways in which the Annunciation provides the backdrop for the entire Advent and Christmas story. The angel's message set in motion that which could not be stopped. God chose to act through Mary of Nazareth, and once Mary had agreed, the die had been cast.

Could Mary have refused?

Adam Hamilton discusses this possibility but instead focuses on Mary's absolute obedience to the angel's words. This raises another question:

Can human beings stifle God's plans and intentions?

Put another way, could Moses or David or Gideon or Paul—or even Jesus—have said no to God?

Can we say no to God? More precisely, do we ever say no to God? How and in what ways? What is God's response?

What can we learn from Mary's complete willingness to serve as God had called her to serve—even in the face of stern retribution from the community?

Closing Prayer

Invite group members to join you in this closing prayer. You may want to copy this prayer on the board, then "line it out" by asking group members to repeat a phrase after you.

Lord God, I want my prayer to be,
"Let it be with me according to your word,"
but so often my own wants and desires get in the way.
I have not been the Christ-bearer you have called me to be.
I have not loved my sisters and brothers
as you have instructed me to love.
I have not forgiven, I have not reconciled,
I have not worked for peace.
But still you have filled me with your grace,
and you continually demonstrate your love for me.
May I experience your forgiveness, Lord,
as I make my way through this time of preparation,
so that I may fully commit myself to the Prince of Peace,
our Savior, Christ Jesus our Lord.
It is in his name that I pray.
Amen.

2.

Joseph of Bethlehem

Getting Started

Session Goals

This session is intended to help participants

- Trace some of the history of Bethlehem through the Old Testament
- Describe the roots of Joseph in Bethlehem, including ways in which the history of Bethlehem may have influenced him
- Draw a word picture of the man Joseph, including his profession, his character, and his faith
- Reflect on some of the claims God makes upon us, including claims that may seem strange or contrary to our traditions and expectations using Joseph as an example

Opening Prayer

The following prayer, taken from Psalm 51, seems to suggest the kind of humility shown by Joseph, as well as his commitment to righteousness and mercy. This particular psalm is said to have been written by King David (an ancestor of Joseph!) when David knew that his sin with Bathsheba had been discovered.

Create in me a clean heart, O God,
and put a new and right spirit within me.

Do not cast me away from your presence,
and do not take your holy spirit from me.
Restore to me the joy of your salvation,
and sustain in me a willing spirit. . . .
O Lord, open my lips,
and my mouth will declare your praise.
Amen.

(Psalm 51:10-12, 15)

Biblical Foundation

Now the birth of Jesus the Messiah took place this way. When his mother Mary had been engaged to Joseph, but before they lived together, she was found to be with child from the Holy Spirit. Her husband Joseph, being a righteous man and unwilling to expose her to public disgrace, planned to dismiss her quietly. But just when he had resolved to do this, an angel of the Lord appeared to him in a dream and said, "Joseph, son of David, do not be afraid to take Mary as your wife, for the child conceived in her is from the Holy Spirit. She will bear a son, and you are to name him Jesus, for he will save his people from their sins." All this took place to fulfill what had been spoken by the Lord through the prophet: "Look, the virgin shall conceive and bear a son and they shall name him Emmanuel," which means "God is with us." When Joseph awoke from sleep, he did as the angel of the Lord commanded him; he took her as his wife. (Matthew 1:18-24)

Opening Activity

In teams of four, share ideas and thoughts about Joseph, the husband of Mary, that team members may have had before reading Chapter 2 of *The Journey* for this session.

- What images of Joseph did team members have? Where did these images originate? Can team members recall Christmas story books that may have been read or heard as children that helped shape their images of Joseph?
- In these images of Joseph, was he a young man, an elderly man, or perhaps a man in his middle ages?

Still working in teams of four, share how these early images of Joseph may have changed or broadened as a result of reading Chapter 2 of *The Journey*. Did they discover any new images of Joseph? How did the book "flesh out" childhood images of Joseph?

Answer this question in the teams of four: How has your image of Joseph changed: from that of a passive observer at the birth of Jesus, to an active participant in the raising of this child?

Reassemble the larger group, and if any of the teams have questions or insights as a result of their discussions, invite them to share these quickly with the whole group.

Learning Together

Video Presentation

Show the video. Be sure all can see clearly; adjust the volume as necessary. As always, be ready to stop the video and replay any portions requested by group members.

(A word of caution: If your group includes people who have been to the Holy Land, use them as a resource but do not let them "get ahead" of the group. For example, they may want to describe the Church of the Nativity during this discussion of Bethlehem; help them realize that this would be more appropriate at a later session.)

Sights
- The town of Bethlehem
- The shepherds' fields surrounding Bethlehem
- The location of Bethlehem relative to Nazareth, Jerusalem, and other significant sites
- The all-important water sources in Bethlehem
- Images of Joseph, such as crèche figures
- Simple hand tools and the honest hard work such tools convey
- The Herodium dominating the view from Bethlehem
- The lavishness of the Herodium contrasted with the humble village of Bethlehem

Insights

- Bethlehem had a long and significant history, having been the home of David, arguably Israel's greatest king.
- Under Roman domination, Bethlehem was simply a small and relatively insignificant town, basically a farming community on the outskirts of a major city.
- The citizens of Bethlehem, knowing the words of Micah and the other prophets, must have wondered if and when Bethlehem would again be restored to glory.
- Bethlehem, like all towns and citizens in Palestine, was dependent on a consistent supply of good water; their water source went back to the time of David and before.
- The citizens of Bethlehem may have been proud of their agricultural produce, living up to the meaning of their town's name—Bethlehem, "House of Bread."
- While the popular image of Joseph is that of a carpenter, he was more accurately a builder, probably working with stone and other materials as well as with wood. Nonetheless, he was a craftsman who worked with his hands and probably received his day's pay each evening like other laborers.
- Justice is not righteousness; mercy is righteousness. Humility is not weakness; humility is ultimate strength.

Group Discussion

- What did you learn about Bethlehem from this video that you had not known before?
- How did the town of Bethlehem help shape Joseph?
- What effect did living in the shadow of the Herodium have on the citizens of Bethlehem?
- Bethlehem is the city of David; what might Herod have been trying to say by constructing his palace overlooking Bethlehem?
- Think for a moment: Is the figure of Joseph in your crèche the figure of an old man? a young man? a man of uncertain age? How might the age of Joseph have influenced the child Jesus?

- Why do you think Joseph isn't mentioned more often in the Gospels? Do you think this omission indicates that, as Jesus grew older, Joseph ceased to be an influence on him? Or does it indicate, as some traditions believe, that Joseph died before Jesus began his public ministry?

Book Study and Discussion

The Scriptures give us many facts about Bethlehem and about Mary, as well as some information about Joseph. But the Scriptures seldom dwell on the feelings and emotions of the people discussed. As the group ponders the questions below, ask them to think with their hearts as well as with their heads. Invite them to put aside for the moment the outcomes that they know took place and instead to try to live in the moment with the biblical characters.

Divide the group into three teams. Each team will consider in some detail an aspect of Chapter 2. Each team's discussion will be guided by a series of questions. (You may copy the questions on the board or jot the questions on a pad of paper that you can give to the team.) Toward the end of the session, each team will report to the whole group about its discussions.

The first team will deal with geography, using these questions:
- What is the significance of Joseph's being of the house of David and being a citizen of Bethlehem, the city of David? How much time elapsed between the time of David and the time of Joseph? (Hint: David's reign as king of Israel is usually dated at about 1000 B.C.)
- How do you think growing up and living in the city of David helped to shape Joseph?
- What effect do you think living in Bethlehem, the "House of Bread," had on Joseph and others living there?
- How might living in the shadow of the Herodium have affected the citizens of Bethlehem?
- If Joseph lived in Bethlehem and Mary lived in Nazareth, how do you think they may have come to be betrothed, a

relationship quite similar to being engaged to be married in our day?

- Do you think arranged marriages are more or less likely to succeed? Give reasons for your answers.

The second team will focus on Joseph, using these questions:

- As a person whom we might call a "blue-collar worker" or manual laborer, what might Joseph's strengths have been? What might his weaknesses have been? Can we know?
- What evidence, if any, do we have that Joseph was a practicing religious person prior to his encounter with the angel in the dream?
- How might Joseph have felt when he learned of Mary's pregnancy? As the offended party, what were his options?
- Why do you think Joseph decided to proceed with his marriage to Mary? What did his choice say about Mary? What did his choice say about Joseph?
- Do you see Joseph as a very young man, perhaps in his teens? as a very old man, perhaps in his nineties? or somewhere in between? Give reasons for your answer. How might Joseph's response to Mary have been different at each of these different ages, and why?
- What kind of humble strength do you think Joseph may have derived from his decision to marry Mary?

The third team will focus on Scripture, dealing with these questions:

- What is the relationship between Isaiah, Chapter 7, and the birth of Jesus?
- How does Adam Hamilton explain the relationship between these biblical passages? What other perspectives or insights can you offer?
- Hamilton suggests that the child of Isaiah, Chapter 7, is Isaiah's son. What are your thoughts and insights on this issue, and why?

- How has the church over the centuries interpreted the connection between Jesus' birth and Isaiah, Chapter 7? What is the difference, if any, between referring to the mother-to-be of Isaiah, Chapter 7, as a virgin or as a young woman?

Call the teams back together and ask for a brief report from each team. Encourage the listening teams to ask questions for clarification of each team's report.

Reflection
- Name and describe some of the times when people in the Bible were influenced by dreams. Do you think the dreams were never/sometimes/always from God? Why or why not?
- Do you think there are different categories and types of dreams? What are the types, and what do you think is the meaning or lack of meaning for each?
- Have you ever had a dream that made a difference in your life? Describe the dream and the difference it made, if you feel comfortable doing so.
- Do you, like Adam Hamilton, have "day dreams"? How are these different from night dreams? Share some of your day dreams, if you would like to.
- Do you believe God speaks to us in day dreams and night dreams? Why or why not?

Bible Study and Discussion
Ask a group member to read Matthew 1:18-25 aloud for the whole group. Encourage the reader to add appropriate expression to the reading in order to help group members experience more of what Joseph was feeling. As a group, consider the following questions:
- How do you imagine Joseph learned of Mary's pregnancy? Did Mary tell him? Did someone else tell him? Might Elizabeth and Zechariah have told him? How do you think Joseph felt on learning this fact?

- Joseph experienced an angel in a dream. How did Joseph know that this was an angel? an angel from God? How would you feel if you dreamed of an angel telling you to do something contrary to popular custom and perhaps contrary to what you were feeling?
- Which of the angel's pronouncements might have surprised Joseph more: that the child was conceived by the Holy Spirit, or that the child would save his people from sin? Explain your answers.
- What is the primary lesson for us to learn about Joseph and his part in the birth of Jesus the Christ?

Wrapping Up

Bring the session to a close by asking group members to describe new insights or learnings they acquired from their study and discussion of Chapter 2. Jot these new insights or learnings on the board. If any group members have lingering questions or concerns, list these also and try to discover appropriate answers or responses for these.

Closing Prayer

The closing prayer is taken from Psalm 33, a psalm that praises all that God has done, is doing, and will continue to do. You may pray this psalm in the name of the group, or you may invite the group to pray this psalm aloud with you.

> *Rejoice in the LORD, O you righteous.*
> *Praise befits the upright.*
> *Praise the LORD with the lyre;*
> *make melody to him with the harp of ten*
> *strings. . . .*
> *For the word of the LORD is upright,*
> *and all his work is done in faithfulness.*

He loves righteousness and justice;
> *the earth is full of the steadfast love of the*
> LORD. . . .
Our soul waits for the LORD;
> *he is our help and shield.*
Our heart is glad in him,
> *because we trust in his holy name.*
Let your steadfast love, O LORD, *be upon us,*
> *even as we hope in you.*
> *Amen.*
> *(Psalm 33:1-2, 4-5, 20-22)*

3.

Mary's Visit to Elizabeth

Getting Started

Session Goals

This session is intended to help participants

- Tell the story of Mary's visit to Elizabeth, including some knowledge of what Mary sought from Elizabeth and what Elizabeth was able to provide for Mary
- Identify and describe the *Magnificat* and its use through the centuries
- Apply the experience of Mary and Elizabeth to contemporary times, especially in terms of seeking support from and acting as a mentor
- Make a commitment to live out the words of the *Magnificat*

Opening Prayer

Our opening prayer is taken from Psalm 31. This psalm praises God's deliverance from enemies, both human and spiritual. This is the kind of psalm that Mary might have sung when she discovered she was pregnant out of wedlock. This psalm puts trust in God ahead of everything else, even though friends and relatives have doubted, rejected, and betrayed. While we may not have faced exactly what Mary faced, all of us have at times felt rejected by friends and loved ones. So this psalm is also our psalm and our prayer:

In you, O LORD, I seek refuge;
do not let me ever be put to shame;
in your righteousness deliver me.
Incline your ear to me;
rescue me speedily.
Be a rock of refuge for me,
a strong fortress to save me. . . .
I am the scorn of all my adversaries,
a horror to my neighbors,
an object of dread to my acquaintances;
those who see me on the street flee from
me. . . .
But I trust in you, O LORD;
I say, "You are my God."
My times are in your hand;
deliver me from the hand of my enemies
and persecutors.
Let your face shine upon your servant;
save me in your steadfast love.
Amen.
(Psalm 31:1-2, 11, 14-16)

Biblical Foundation

In those days Mary set out and went with haste to a Judean town in the hill country, where she entered the house of Zechariah and greeted Elizabeth. When Elizabeth heard Mary's greeting, the child leaped in her womb. And Elizabeth was filled with the Holy Spirit and exclaimed with a loud cry, "Blessed are you among women, and blessed is the fruit of your womb. And why has this happened to me, that the mother of my Lord comes to me? For as soon as I heard the sound of your greeting, the child in my womb leaped for joy. And blessed is she who believed that there would be a fulfillment of what was spoken to her by the Lord."

Mary said, "My soul magnifies the Lord, and my spirit rejoices in God my Savior, for he has looked with favor on the lowliness of his servant. Surely, from now on all generations will call me blessed; for the Mighty One has done great things for me, and holy is his name. His mercy is for those who fear him from generation to generation. He has shown strength with his arm; he has scattered the proud in the thoughts of their hearts. He has brought down the powerful from their thrones, and lifted up the lowly; he has filled the hungry with good things, and sent the rich away empty. He has helped his servant Israel, in remembrance of his mercy, according to the promise he made to our ancestors, to Abraham and to his descendants forever."

And Mary remained with her about three months and then returned to her home. (Luke 1:39-56)

Opening Activity

Invite two women in your group who are good readers to read aloud Luke 1:42-55. Encourage them to read with expression and appropriate gestures. If your group includes people of various ages, selecting an older woman and a younger woman for these two parts would be ideal.

To add some additional meaning and insight to this dialogue, you might ask the women to read first from the New Revised Standard Version of the Bible, then to read this passage again from another translation, perhaps the Common English Bible or the New International Version.

Ask group members to comment on new insights or understandings gained from hearing these passages read from different translations.

Learning Together

Video Presentation

Make sure that all can see the video screen clearly and that the volume is adjusted so that all can hear. Play the video, but be prepared to stop or to replay sections of the video at the request of group members.

Sights

- A map showing the locations of Nazareth and Ein Karem, the traditional home of Zechariah and Elizabeth
- The Palestinian countryside showing the contours of the land over which Mary had to travel to visit Elizabeth
- The church built over the grotto, the traditional home of Zechariah and Elizabeth, and the birthplace of John the Baptist
- Symbolic representations of Mary and Elizabeth in the courtyard of the church
- An exterior wall of the church displaying the words of the *Magnificat* in many different languages
- Faces of need, especially children, both at home and abroad

Insights

- Mary's anguish at her condition and her need of someone she could talk to whom she could trust
- Mary's determination to visit Elizabeth, despite an arduous nine- or ten-day journey
- Elizabeth's immediate acceptance of Mary and her condition, and Elizabeth's constant encouragement
- The need for older mentors and the related need to serve as mentors for those who are younger
- The various affirmations contained within the *Magnificat*, including the call to all who serve those in need of any kind
- The many opportunities to serve those in need, both locally and across the globe
- The eagerness of most people to serve others in need if and when such opportunities are presented

Group Discussion

Invite group members to form teams of three, in which they will discuss responses to the questions below. Working in small teams gives everyone a chance to participate.

- Why do you think Mary was so anxious to visit Elizabeth that she traveled nine or ten days over very rough terrain, risking possible danger to herself and her unborn baby?

- Do you think that Mary sent word to Elizabeth in advance of her visit? Do you think Elizabeth knew of Mary's pregnancy before Mary arrived? Give some reasons for your responses, but realize that these are hypothetical questions; Scripture does not provide answers.
- Watching the video, we learn that Mary cared for Elizabeth during the latter's third trimester of pregnancy even as Elizabeth cared for Mary during Mary's first trimester. What do you think Mary did for Elizabeth, and what do you think Elizabeth did for Mary? Again, realize that this is conjecture; Scripture does not provide clear answers.
- How can we literally fill the hungry with good things? In what ways are people hungry today? Is hunger always for food? What other things might people hunger for?

Gather the larger group once more, and ask for brief reports from the teams of three. Did most of the teams respond to the questions in similar ways? Why or why not?

Book Study and Discussion

Though in Chapter 3 Adam Hamilton focuses on the relationship between Mary and Elizabeth and retells the story of Mary's visit to her relative's home and her three-month stay there, he touches more significantly on three other areas of interest that grow out of this visit. Rather than telling and retelling the story of the long trip and the visit, focus instead on these three other areas.

Divide into three teams and encourage each team to probe deeply into questions about one of the three areas.

Team One

What does it mean to be blessed? Elizabeth called Mary blessed three times, but Mary probably did not feel very blessed, at least blessed in the traditional sense of great good fortune.

- What does being blessed by God mean to us today?

- Do we tend to equate being blessed with good fortune?
- How does the author define being blessed by God?
- In what ways have you seen others blessed in the sense that the author discusses?
- In what ways do you feel that you have been blessed in the unique way that the author describes?

Team Two

Adam Hamilton places great emphasis on our need for mentors and to mentor in return. He describes in some detail some of his significant mentors.

- Who has served as a mentor for you? Let all the team members describe quickly mentors who helped shape and form them.
- Did Mary go to Elizabeth expecting to be mentored, or did the mentoring relationship simply emerge on its own? Ask team members to describe experiences they have had of serving as a mentor for a younger person. Did the group member choose to be a mentor—or did this relationship simply emerge?
- Organizations such as Big Brothers and Big Sisters, the Boys and Girls Club, and scouting groups seek to provide mentors for young people. How can team members become more active in serving as mentors for the young?

Team Three

The *Magnificat* emphasizes how God has lifted the lowly and filled the hungry with good things. In his book, Adam Hamilton emphasizes that this is a charge for each of us, that each of us as a disciple is called to lift the lowly and fill the hungry with good things. In the video presentation, Hamilton describes what his church is doing to lift the lowly and feed the hungry.

- As a team, describe and discuss some of the many ways you can lift the lowly and feed the hungry. Do not limit your discussion to taking monetary offerings; this is perhaps the least personal and easiest thing to do. Instead, focus on the many, many other ways in which you as a team, as a study group, and as individual disciples of Christ Jesus can lift the lowly and feed the hungry. (Hint: Remember the earlier discussion of the many ways in which persons hunger—in addition to being hungry for physical food.)

- Ask all team members to jot down on a small slip of paper—for their eyes only!—at least three ways they will seek in the coming week to lift the lowly and feed the hungry. Suggest that each team member carry that slip of paper in pocket or purse throughout the week as a reminder of this special call to be blessed by being a blessing for others.

If time permits, ask for a report from each of the teams. Entertain questions from any of the teams, and encourage the whole group to struggle with these questions.

Reflection
- How would you define *joy*? How is *joy* different from *happiness*?
- Have you ever experienced joy and at the same time felt unhappy? Have you ever felt happy but not joyful? If you have experienced these feelings, describe them and the circumstances.
- Have you ever felt joyful in difficult or even painful circumstances, as with Mary's unexpected pregnancy or Paul's imprisonment?
- Think about the phrase "magnifies the Lord." What does it mean? Is it possible to magnify the Lord? Why or why not?

Bible Study and Discussion
Though Mary is one of the main characters described in the Scripture for this session, it is Elizabeth who recognizes the uniqueness of Mary's offspring. In fact. Elizabeth's unborn child

recognizes that Mary's unborn child is the Lord, and Elizabeth's child—to be John the Baptist—leaps with excitement in Elizabeth's womb. This leads Elizabeth to hail Mary as blessed over and over again and to call Mary the mother of Elizabeth's—and the universe's!—Lord.

Do you think Mary grasped the significance of all of this? Was Mary clinging to the words of the angel's message? Or did those words fade somewhat as Mary faced what could have been the terrible consequences of being found pregnant out of wedlock? Though the Scriptures do not provide us with these details, challenge group members to ponder the questions in order to gain greater insight into Mary and Elizabeth.

Wrapping Up

This session has opened many new ideas including but also beyond the simple story of Mary's visit with her relative Elizabeth. Invite the participants to share a moment of silence as each group member reflects on a new learning or a new insight that emerged from the book, video, Scripture passage, and/or discussion. Then ask group members to share that new learning with one other group member. After a few minutes, ask each pair to join another pair to exchange new insights and understandings.

Closing Prayer

The closing prayer for this session is taken, not from the Book of Psalms, but from Isaiah, Chapter 58. The words of Isaiah have been adapted into prayer form. You may read the prayer for the group, line it out for the group, or post it on the board so group members can offer this prayer aloud together:

Lord God, you have called us,
each of us,
to loose the bonds of injustice,

to let the oppressed go free,
and to break every yoke.
You have called us to share our bread with the hungry,
to bring the homeless poor into our houses,
and to cover the naked.
Almighty God, in the words of Mary's Magnificat,
may we magnify the Lord who calls us to do these things,
and may we do them joyfully and thankfully.
We pray this prayer in the name of Christ Jesus.
Amen.

4.

From Nazareth to Bethlehem

Getting Started

Session Goals

This session is intended to help participants

- Consider the possible route taken by Mary and Joseph from Nazareth to Bethlehem, including its length and difficulty
- Reflect on the condition of Mary and Joseph as they undertook this trek
- Ponder and identify in their own lives the theme of journey as a metaphor for life

Opening Prayer

Because the motif of journey is so pronounced in this session, verses from Psalm 139 seem especially appropriate as an opening prayer. The psalmist assures us that wherever the journey of life takes us, God is with us. You may read this psalm prayer for the group or copy it on the board and invite the group to offer this prayer aloud.

O LORD, . . .
Where can I go from your spirit?
Or where can flee I from your presence?

If I ascend to heaven, you are there;
    if I make my bed in Sheol, you are there.
If I take the wings of the morning
    and settle at the farthest limits of the sea,
even there your hand shall lead me,
    and your right hand shall hold me fast. . . .
Search me, O God, and know my heart;
    test me and know my thoughts.
See if there is any wicked way in me,
    and lead me in the way everlasting.
    Amen.
                (Psalm 139:7-10, 23-24)

Biblical Foundation

In those days a decree went out from Emperor Augustus that all the world should be registered. This was the first registration and was taken while Quirinius was governor of Syria. All went to their own towns to be registered. Joseph also went from the town of Nazareth in Galilee to Judea, to the city of David called Bethlehem, because he was descended from the house and family of David. He went to be registered with Mary, to whom he was engaged and who was expecting a child. While they were there, the time came for her to deliver her child. And she gave birth to her firstborn son and wrapped him in bands of cloth, and laid him in a manger, because there was no place for them in the inn. (Luke 2:1-7)

Opening Activity

One of the recurrent themes in Chapter 4 is the motif of journey. The author uses this motif to remind us that all of life is a journey, and just as Mary and Joseph were greatly affected by the journey from Nazareth to Bethlehem, so we are often changed dramatically by a journey or journeys in our lives.

Divide the group into teams of three, and ask the teams to discuss the following questions briefly. As some situations might be very personal, do not press for responses but encourage all to share in some ways, either by describing their own journeys or by helping others describe their journeys.

- When in your life did a journey radically alter your life?
- Was this a journey you wanted to take, or was it required of you?
- Did you take the journey alone or in the company of someone else—a loved one? a friend? a stranger?
- Some life-changing journeys cover thousands of miles; others cover only a block or two, or even a few feet. What was the case with your journey?
- How were you changed by the journey; how was your life made different?
- How did you feel about this journey once it was ended? Were you glad to have taken it? sorry to have taken it? Why?

(Hint: If group members have trouble getting started, remind them of the journey to a new school, the journey down the aisle in marriage, the journey to a job interview, the journey into military service, and so on.)

Learning Together

Video Presentation

Before showing the video, urge group members to use their imaginations to experience the video with all their senses. In addition to seeing the images and hearing the voice of the presenter, what else does the video suggest the viewers might sense if they were in the Holy Land with Adam Hamilton? Can they see hawks flying high over the hills of Judea? Can they hear the wind whistling through the trees? Can they feel the stones under their feet? Can they feel the heat of the sun? Can they smell the green of the leaves on the olive trees? Can they smell the cool dampness of the areas around Jacob's Well? Can they taste the cool water from Jacob's Well? the interesting sweetness of the carob? the grit of the sand in their mouths in the Judean wilderness? Encourage group members to experience this video and all videos with all their senses.

Play the video; as always, be ready to stop and replay parts of the video if group members request that you do so. Following the video presentation, invite group members to describe some of the ways they experienced the video with all their senses.

Sights

- A map showing possible routes taken by Mary and Joseph
- The Way of the Patriarchs, one of these routes that passes through Samaria
- The Jezreel Valley, including modern roads and high-speed traffic
- The Valley of Meggido
- The pathway through what is now part of the West Bank
- Groves of olive trees
- Carob trees growing naturally around sources of water
- The modern city of Sychar
- Jacob's Well and the church built over it
- The mountainous landscape around the approach to Bethlehem
- The way of the Jordan River
- The Judean wilderness in all its bleak beauty

Insights

- The difficulty of the journey for Joseph and Mary, especially given Mary's condition
- The probable reluctance on the part of Mary and Joseph to take the journey, but the legal requirement that they do so
- Again, the importance of potable water throughout Palestine, as evidenced in stops between Nazareth and Bethlehem in places where water was available
- The metaphor of journey and the application of this metaphor to much of life

Group Discussion

Invite a brief discussion by the whole group around some or all the following questions, based on the video presentation.

- What things did you see in the video that surprised you or were new to you? How did these things help you understand the journey by Joseph and Mary more completely?
- What new insights into Mary and Joseph's journey emerged as a result of watching the video?
- Imagine yourself walking about eighty miles over the terrain you saw in the video. What preparations for the journey would you make? What would you take with you? What special preparations and supplies might you take if you were accompanied by a loved one who was about to give birth?
- How would you feel if you were required to make this arduous a journey at the demand of an occupying power?

Book Study and Discussion

In the book, Adam Hamilton fills in many details about the relationships among Elizabeth, Joseph, and Mary. He speculates that Joseph, living in Bethlehem, was informed of Mary's pregnancy, chose to marry her nonetheless, and returned with her to Nazareth for the wedding, as was the custom of the day. Hamilton also suggests that Mary and Joseph went to Nazareth about the third or fourth month of Mary's pregnancy and that they were formally married about the sixth month of Mary's pregnancy. As he points out, the custom of the day was for a married couple to reside with the groom's parents until the groom was able to provide housing on his own.

While none of these details can be found in Scripture, enough is known about the customs of the time to make some very educated guesses. Thus, in the course of about nine months, Mary made three difficult journeys: to Elizabeth's home near Bethlehem, back to Nazareth for her wedding, and a return to Bethlehem on the occasion of the Roman census. As suggested, each of these journeys required about ten days of travel; and due to Mary's pregnancy each was more difficult for her than the previous one.

- As a group, ponder and discuss what may have been Mary's frame of mind throughout this time. Do you think she was excited? resigned? angry and frustrated? thankful? worried and anxious?
- Recall that Mary had been visited by the angel at the Annunciation, but there had been no more direct contact with the angel after that. Mary's offspring had been recognized as holy by Elizabeth—and Elizabeth probably reinforced that idea during Mary's three-month stay with her—but would that visit and reinforcement have been enough to give Mary complete confidence in all that was about to transpire?
- Joseph had had a remarkable dream, and because of that dream he had committed himself to Mary, no matter what. But would even Joseph's dream have been enough to assure Mary that all would be well, that she was surely doing God's will? Remember that Mary may have been as young as thirteen and may not have been literate, as the custom of the day provided schooling only for boys. And then Joseph told Mary, just as she was about to deliver her child, that they must trek back to Bethlehem again. Put yourself in Mary's shoes: How would you have felt?

Adam Hamilton mentions the noncanonical books that identify Mary's parents and provide other information about the journey to Bethlehem, such as the use of a donkey. These books, written some time after the events took place, were not recognized by the early church councils that established the canon (the books to be included in the New Testament).

As a group, discuss briefly some of the reasons why these books might have been written, especially as much as a hundred years after the fact. Recognize that we are hungry for more details, more information, more insight into those things we consider sacred and holy, those things that transform our lives. Thus, such books were written to round out the story, to fill in details, to give us more information about things in which we are vitally interested. Help group members recognize that these books and the stories they present are not necessarily wrong or incorrect but are conjectures indicating what might have taken place.

Divide into teams of four and quickly review the section of the book titled Room in the Inn? The innkeeper is such a standard character in Nativity dramas that most of us have grown up with the understanding that Joseph and Mary went to a commercial establishment to find lodging.

- What is Adam Hamilton's belief about this?
- Hamilton speculates that the guest rooms in Joseph's family home were so crowded and the taboos about ritual purity so great that Mary and Joseph were given a place in the family stable. If this was so, what might it say about Mary and Joseph?
- Do you think that Mary and Joseph might have been ostracized by Joseph's family because of Mary's pregnancy?
- Alternatively, do you think that Mary and Joseph might have volunteered to spend the night in the stable rather than force other family members to surrender the guest rooms in which they were already established? Give reasons for your answer.
- How does your answer affect your understanding of the traditional Christmas story?

Invite group members to raise points or questions about other parts of this chapter in the book. The chapter is rich in detail, and though some of it is admittedly speculation, it forces new thinking and response about the story of the Nativity.

Reflection
- One of Adam Hamilton's themes in *The Journey* is the importance of our response to God's call. Have you ever experienced God's call? What form did it take?
- If you have experienced God's call, how have you responded? What forms do you think such responses can take?

- Cite some examples of God's call in the Bible and in the world. How did these people respond? What can we learn from their responses?
- List some projects in your area and in the world that could constitute a response by you to God's call. What are some initial steps you could take to follow up?

Bible Study and Discussion

In teams of four people each, consider some or all of the following questions:

- Why do you think Luke was so specific about the dating of the decree? Remember to whom Luke was writing; why would careful dating of the decree be of interest to them?
- Why in verse 4 does Luke emphasize Joseph's ancestry? Why was Joseph's relationship to King David (about one thousand years earlier!) so important to Luke? What did this relationship say about the child Mary was about to bear?
- Why does Luke emphasize that Joseph and Mary were engaged and that she was about to bear her firstborn?
- What new insights into the story of the Nativity have you gained from the book, the video presentation, and the group's discussions? Will any of these new insights change or affect the way you think about and celebrate Christmas? If so, how?

Wrapping Up

Return to the theme of journey as a metaphor for life. Ask group members to ponder the following questions in silence, answering for themselves but not sharing their responses with anyone else.

- How did the journey from Nazareth to Bethlehem change and define the lives of Mary and Joseph?
- How have journeys in your life changed and defined your life?

- What journeys are you facing now that may alter and define your life?
- The journey of Mary and Joseph demonstrated that God was with them. How do you experience God being with you as you journey through life and as you face significant journeys ahead?

Closing Prayer

With the theme of journey still fresh in mind, you might remind the group of lines from William Cullen Bryant's poem, "To a Waterfowl." Addressing the waterfowl, Bryant writes,

> He, who, from zone to zone
> Guides through the boundless sky thy certain flight,
> In the long way that I must tread alone,
> Will lead my steps aright.

The following prayer is adapted from Psalm 46, a psalm that reminds us that God is with us in all our journeys:

Almighty God, you are our refuge and strength, a very present help in trouble. Therefore we will not fear, though the earth should change, though the mountains shake in the heart of the sea; though its waters roar and foam, though the mountains tremble with its tumult. Lord of hosts, you are with us. You are our refuge. Thanks be to God. We offer this prayer in the name of Christ Jesus. Amen.

5.

The Manger

Getting Started

Session Goals

This session is intended to help participants

- Paint a word picture of the spot that tradition reports Christ was born
- Reflect on the meaning of the site chosen for the birth of the Messiah
- Ponder the long-range meaning of the conditions of the Messiah's birth
- Discuss the meanings of both the visit of the shepherds and the visit of the magi
- Reach new and significant understandings of God's will for humankind as reflected in the Incarnation, the Word made flesh

Opening Prayer

Our opening prayer consists of selected verses from Psalm 30, adapted as a prayer. This psalm praises God for God's infinite goodness, a goodness made manifest in the birth, life, death, and resurrection of Christ Jesus. As with the other opening prayers, you may read it aloud for the group or copy it on the board so group members may pray aloud in unison.

We will extol you, Lord, for you have drawn us up and did not let our foes rejoice over us. O Lord, we cried to you for help and you have healed us. Therefore, let us sing praises to the Lord and give thanks to his holy name. For his anger is but for a moment; his favor for a lifetime. Our weeping may linger for the night, but joy comes with the morning. Our souls will praise you, Lord, and not be silent. O Lord our God, we will give thanks to you forever. Amen.

Biblical Foundation

In that region there were shepherds living in the fields keeping watch over their flock by night. Then an angel of the Lord stood before them, and the glory of the Lord shone around them, and they were terrified. But the angel said to them, "Do not be afraid; for see—I am bringing you good news of great joy for all the people: to you is born this day in the city of David a Savior, who is the Messiah, the Lord. This will be a sign for you: you will find a child wrapped in bands of cloth and lying in a manger."And suddenly there was with the angel a multitude of the heavenly host praising God and saying, "Glory to God in the highest heaven, and on earth peace among those whom he favors!"

When the angels had left them and gone into heaven, the shepherds said to one another, "Let us go now to Bethlehem and see this thing that has taken place, which the Lord has made known to us." So they went with haste and found Mary and Joseph and the child lying in a manger. When they saw this, they made known what had been told them about this child; and all who heard it were amazed at what the shepherds told them. But Mary treasured all these words and pondered them in her heart. The shepherds returned, glorifying and praising God for all they had heard and seen, as it had been told them. (Luke 2:8-20)

Opening Activity

Our study reaches its destination this week as we read about Mary giving birth to the Messiah, to Jesus the Christ. Everything else in the story has taken place so that this moment might be. All has been preparation; the promise, the dream, the hope is now fulfilled as the Christ Child is born.

In teams of four people each, let all the team members describe two experiences: (1) the ways in which they or their families celebrate—not Christmas, but the birth of the Christ Child; (2) the appearance of any crèche or Nativity figures in their homes. What does the form and style, the plainness or elaborateness of the crèche say about the birth of the Christ Child? This is not a time for judgment, to critique one another's family celebrations or manger scenes. It is instead a time to demonstrate the variety of ways in which this most significant birth is recognized and celebrated, not in churches but in homes.

Learning Together

Video Presentation
Prepare to show the video. As you did in previous sessions, invite group members to experience the video with all their senses. What sounds, sights, and smells may have filled the place as Jesus was born? Our usual tradition is that Jesus was born in a barn and placed in a wooden manger with X-shaped legs. Would the anticipated sights, sounds, and smells in such a place be the same as—or different from—the sights, sounds, and smells that would accompany a birth in the grotto of a cave, as demonstrated on the video?

Show the video, and be prepared to replay any portions of the video that group members might request.

Sights
- Modern Bethlehem
- Caves around Bethlehem, still used by the Bedouin
- The floor plan of a first-century dwelling in Bethlehem
- Manger Square in Bethlehem
- The Church of the Nativity
- The Door of Humility leading into the Church of the Nativity
- The rich interior of the Church of the Nativity
- The grotto under the altar of the Church of the Nativity
- The spot, marked by a fourteen-point silver star, said to be where Christ was born

- The Chapel of the Manger, where it is said the infant Christ was placed after his birth
- A stone manger, typical of this first-century period
- The shepherds' fields
- A modern shepherd with his sheep

If any members of your group have been to the Holy Land, invite them at this point to describe the Church of the Nativity and the grotto in which Christ was born. Encourage them to identify in some detail their feelings as they descended the handful of stairs into the grotto and their feelings as they looked at the place where Christ was born and where the infant was placed immediately after his birth. Ask them also to describe the interior of the Church of the Nativity and the feelings it stirred within them.

Insights
- Tradition has affected but not changed some of the facts we know about the Nativity.
- Every element in the Nativity has a meaning; while the Nativity is not an allegory, the event was carefully and intentionally planned from time immemorial.
- Christians find new meanings and new realities in the elements of the Nativity.
- Luke and Matthew's accounts of the Nativity, while different, are complementary.
- The events of the Nativity demonstrate that Jesus was not simply the Messiah of the Jews but instead the Christ of all humankind.

Group Discussion
- Do you think the many meanings in the Nativity are evidence of God's plan? Are they evidence of reading back into the events on the part of committed Christians? or both? Give reasons for your answers. What difference, if any, is made by choosing one option over the other?

- If these meanings are evidence of God's plan, then do you think God has a detailed plan for each of us?
- If so, how can we know that plan?
- Can we resist or refuse that plan?

Book Study and Discussion

In the book, Adam Hamilton focuses on a number of details surrounding the birth of Jesus. Many of these, such as the Church of the Nativity, are included in the videos too. But the book also discusses several other details that cannot be shown in the videos. Let's turn our attention to these.

In teams of three, invite group members to review that portion of the book that deals with the angel and the angelic chorus. Then ask the teams to discuss the following questions:

- What do angels look like? Must angels be clothed in white and fly on white wings? Are angels the fat little children we see on Valentine cards? If not, then how can we identify angels?
- Are angels still in our midst? How do we know?
- In the Old Testament, the angels who encountered Abraham appeared as ordinary travelers. Might the angel who talked with the shepherds have been, as Hamilton speculates, a stranger who simply walked up to the shepherds in the night and spoke with them?
- If this were the case, might the angelic chorus have appeared as a small group of people who appeared on the hillsides with the shepherds?
- More importantly, might angels appear to us today as very ordinary people with an extraordinary message? As always, give reasons for responding to these questions as you do.

Do not ask for reports from each team, but if any teams have questions or concerns, attend to these.

Another important emphasis in the book is the angels' message: "Good news of great joy for all the people." If your group members can move quickly, divide the larger group into four smaller groups and consider the following questions in the teams:

Team One

- What is the good news that the angels bring? Be specific.
- What does it mean to refer to the one being born as Savior, Messiah, and Lord? Do these three titles mean the same thing or different things? If they are different, what does each mean?
  - Savior—Saved from what for what?
  - Messiah—The Promised One, but what promise does the Messiah fulfill?
  - Lord—What does living under the lordship of Christ Jesus mean? We who live in the United States have never lived under the lordship of anyone; how can we understand the lordship of Christ?

Team Two

- Do you think the shepherds, presumably Jewish, understood "all the people" to mean only Jews?
- Could the angels' phrase have included the Gentiles? the hated Romans?
- What does the phrase "all the people" mean in our day? Does the phrase mean all Christians? all good people? Does the phrase include Muslims? Buddhists? Jews? atheists?
- Does the phrase include those who have no regard for Christ or his will for us? Does it include those who reject the norms of society and break all of society's laws? Does the phrase include those for whom the birth of Christ was not and is not good news? What must a person do to be included in the phrase "all the people"?

Team Three

- What is peace? Is it only the absence of warfare and conflict? If not, then what is the peace that Christ brings?
- Does Christ bring peace only to individuals, or does Christ also bring peace to nations? or both? Give reasons for your answer.
- Once *peace* is defined, then the question becomes: Who are "those" whom God favors? What do you think?

- Is the promised peace to be only for those favored by God? If so, who are the favored? How can people know if they are among the favored? (Hint: Go back and read Luke 2:10 for clues. According to this verse, whom does God favor?)

Team Four
- What did the visit of the magi say to the people who surrounded Mary and Joseph and the infant Jesus?
- What does the visit of the magi say to us?
- What does their visit demonstrate and emphasize?

Reflection
- Think of journeys in your own life that you did not want to take. As you feel comfortable, share the circumstances and the results.
- Beyond your own experiences, describe some journeys, famous or otherwise, that others didn't want to take. What were the results, and what can we learn from those journeys?
- How long should we wait before judging the results of our journeys? Have there been difficult journeys in your own life that might yet turn out to be positive? Are there good results of every journey?

Bible Study and Discussion

Read aloud the Bible passage for this session. Even though it is well known, its words are ever new and exciting. Ask the entire group to consider these questions:
- What happened to the shepherds when the angels left them?
- What did the shepherds do? Did the shepherds hurry to Bethlehem to find out if the angel's statements were true? Or did they go in complete belief in what the angel had said? For what other reasons might they have left their sheep and rushed into the city?
- Just as significantly, what did the shepherds do after they

had seen the Holy Family? Why did the shepherds make known to everyone the things they had seen and heard?

• How do you think the shepherds "made known" what they had seen and heard?

If your group enjoys role playing, ask two or three members to play the part of the shepherds and another two or three to take the part of townspeople. Let the "shepherds" tell the "townspeople" about what they have seen, and let the "townspeople" react as the role players imagine the townspeople may have reacted.

Wrapping Up

Your group has experienced the Nativity in depth. You have seen, read, and learned many details about the birth of Jesus. But the story is not over yet. Just as the shepherds proclaimed to all what they had heard and seen on the hillside and in the manger, so must we as modern-day Christians proclaim to all the message of the angels and the presence of the Christ.

Ask all the group members to jot down on a slip of paper—for their eyes only!—at least five ways they will proclaim the good news in the days and weeks ahead. Ask group members to keep that slip of paper in their pocket, wallet, or purse as a reminder to them to make known what had been told them about this child!

Closing Prayer

Our closing prayer for the session and for the study must be a prayer of pure praise and thanksgiving unto God for all that God has done, is doing, and will do in and through Christ Jesus. Psalm 150 is a psalm of pure praise and thanksgiving. Post this psalm on the board, or line it out so that all can participate in its joyful praise.

Before reading this psalm prayer aloud as a group, remind members that we cannot praise God quietly or passively, we cannot praise God with trumpet sound indifferently, we cannot praise

God with loud, clashing cymbals in hushed, mumbling tones. Encourage group members to offer this prayer aloud as a genuine, heartfelt thanksgiving!

> *Praise the LORD!*
> *Praise God in his sanctuary;*
> > *praise him in his mighty*
> > *firmament!*
> *Praise him for his mighty deeds;*
> > *praise him according to his*
> > *surpassing greatness!*
> *Praise him with trumpet sound;*
> > *praise him with lute and harp!*
> *Praise him with tambourine and dance;*
> > *praise him with strings and pipe!*
> *Praise him with clanging cymbals;*
> > *praise him with loud clashing*
> > *cymbals!*
> *Let everything that breathes praise the*
> > *LORD!*
> *Praise the LORD!*
> > *Amen.*

Churchwide Study of *The Journey*

The Journey: Walking the Road to Bethlehem explores the story of Jesus' birth with fresh eyes and ears in order to discover the real meaning of Christmas. Author Adam Hamilton draws upon insights gained from historians, archaeologists, biblical scholars, and theologians and from walking in the places where the story occurred.

A churchwide Advent program for all ages will help people come to a deeper understanding of what the Christmas story teaches us about Jesus Christ and about God's will for our lives. It will offer opportunities for learning, for intergenerational activities, and for reaching out to the community.

Resources for the Churchwide Study

Adults
The Journey: Walking the Road to Bethlehem – Book
The Journey: A Season of Reflections – Devotional companion
The Journey: DVD - Videos (optional for youth)

Youth
The Journey: Walking the Road to Bethlehem for Youth – Leader guide

Children
The Journey: Walking the Road to Bethlehem for Children – Leader guide

Schedule Suggestions

Many churches have weeknight programs that include an evening meal, an intergenerational gathering time, and classes for children, youth, and adults. The following schedule illustrates one way to organize a weeknight program.

- 5:30 p.m.: Gather for a meal.
- 6:00 p.m.: Have an intergenerational gathering that introduces the subject and primary Scriptures for that evening's session. This time may include presentations, skits, music, and opening or closing prayers.
- 6:15 –8:45 p.m.: Gather in classes for children, youth, and adults.

You may choose to position this study as a Sunday school program. This approach would be similar to the weeknight schedule, except with a shorter class time (which is common for Sunday morning programs). The following schedule takes into account a shorter class time, which is the norm for Sunday morning programs.

- 10 minutes: Have an intergenerational gathering that is similar to the one described above.
- 45 minutes: Gather in classes for children, youth, and adults.

Choose a schedule that works best for your congregation and its existing Christian education programs.

Activity Suggestions

All-Church Art Show
Directions for an art show can be found in each lesson of *The Journey: Walking the Road to Bethlehem for Children*. Instructions for the final art show are in Lesson 5.

All-Church Baby Blanket Drive
Ask participants to bring new baby blankets to give to a homeless shelter, battered women's shelter, or food pantry. If you would like to combine this activity with the previous one, designate the blankets as tickets to enter the art show.

Costumed Greeters
Recruit volunteers to dress up as the biblical characters being studied each week. For the first lesson, recruit an adult or youth to dress as the angel Gabriel. Gabriel should greet each person at the door with the words, "Rejoice, (person's name), favored one. The Lord is with you!" There are scripts and suggestions for each lesson in *The Journey: Walking the Road to Bethlehem for Children*.

An Amazing Race
Divide the participants into intergenerational groups to play "An Amazing Race." The directions for the game are found in Lesson 3 of *The Journey: Walking the Road to Bethlehem for Children*.

A New Christmas Tradition

On Christmas Eve, we invite our congregation to give of what is precious to them as an expression of their joy and gratitude for the birth of Jesus and his role in their lives. For some who are struggling financially, the gift may be something small, but all are invited to give something if they are able. These gifts are then given to projects benefiting children in poverty, divided equally between projects in the developing world (currently Africa) and in our own inner city. This has become one of our most meaningful traditions. Even those who are non-religious find this to be a moving part of the service.

Mike Slaughter, pastor of the Ginghamsburg United Methodist Church, reminds his congregation each year that "Christmas is not your birthday!" Consider giving a special offering this Christmas, for people in need. If you have children, teach your children this tradition, and help them learn that Christmas is not primarily about what is under the tree, but about God's gift of Jesus Christ, and, in turn, Christ's call upon our lives to give ourselves for others.